I DIDN'T KNOW
THAT COMES
FROM THE
BIBLE

Copyright © 2013 by K. Rose Publishing, Inc.

ISBN 978-1-60587-525-5
ISBN 978-1-60587-548-4 (special edition)

Published by Freeman-Smith, a division of Worthy Media, Inc.,
134 Franklin Road, Suite 200, Brentwood, Tennessee 37027.

Library of Congress Control Number: 2013945024

All Scripture quotations, unless otherwise noted, are taken from:

The Holy Bible, King James Version

Cover Design by Kim Russell / Wahoo Designs
Page Layout by Bart Dawson

Printed in the United States of America

1 2 3 4 5—SBI—16 15 14 13

I DIDN'T KNOW THAT COMES FROM THE BIBLE

FROM **SOUR GRAPES** TO **FEET OF CLAY**, BIBLICAL ORIGINS BEHIND EVERYDAY WORDS AND EXPRESSIONS

Karlen Evins

✳FS
FREEMAN-SMITH

FOR A.-J.

TABLE OF CONTENTS

New Testament

ACKNOWLEDGMENTS

In the life cycle of a book, the signings come last. First you write. Then you print. If you're smart, you market and publicize that you have a book. Then you show up for the signings and pray someone buys the book, at which point you sign and say "Thanks!"

This book started with a signing. And most every step hence has come about in reverse order, which makes this one of the more unique projects I've ever worked on.

I was at my first signing for the original *I Didn't Know That*, playing to a hometown crowd, when I launched into what is the fun part of this process: asking the audience for their favorite expressions. When someone shouted out, *Same Ol' Sixes and Sevens*, I made a note to look it up, conceding that I didn't know.

Later, an angel of a soul came up and said, "I'm surprised you didn't know that one with your Div background and all... After all, it's in the Bible."

He shared what he knew, and by the time I got home, I was pulling out the ol' King James, sticking post-its on the book of Job, while noting other passages along the way.

This book began that night thanks to David Pflaum. In addition to sharing his insight on one single expression, we went on to become great friends as our email exchanges birthed a list that would eventually become this book. That David so graciously gave of his time and personal love of Scripture to cross check and edit along the way only adds to my gratitude.

Likewise, I owe a world of thanks to my dear friend and former professor, Amy-Jill Levine, Professor of New Testament Studies at Vanderbilt University. Never has a *trivia* book been taken more seriously (for in truth, there is nothing trivial about Scripture). But in reminding me again and again to "stay true to the text," A.-J. was as tough on this one as she was on me when I was her student. As a result I am a better person for it.

And this is a better book.

My thanks as well to Jonathan Merkh, Mark Gilroy and Troy Johnson for encouraging me to continue this work even when the manuscript was between publishing houses. Even while flying without a net, you reminded me to persevere, focusing on the book itself and not the crazy book business. As a result, things timed out beautifully.

Nothing by chance…

It takes a village to birth a book. Fortunate for me, my village was a city of angels…

To these who were hands on, as well as those who supported me behind the scenes, I say "Thank you." If success is measured by the love we experience along the way, then this book is a success already, for the joy was truly in the journey.

With heartfelt thanks,

Karlen Evins

A NOTE FROM THE AUTHOR

With a Southern Baptist mother and a Church of Christ dad, I grew up in the buckle of the Bible belt. Life around our house wasn't always peaceful, but we kids did know our Scripture.

I was baptized into two religions: once at age six; again at age twelve (just in case the first one didn't take). I attended a lot of Bible Schools in my summer months, and the rest of the year found me in church twice on Sundays, once on Wednesday nights, and in chapel on Fridays (because it was mandatory where I went to school).

We take our religion very seriously where I come from, but no matter your faith, most of us hold sacred the traditions we grew up with and the phrases we've come to love (some of which jump right off the Bible pages and into our everyday conversations).

My career began in advertising. But as fate (or God) would have it, I wound up a talk show host, whose daily fare included politics and all things "hard news." But through it all, my growing up years stayed with me.

In attempts to mesh my fundamentalist up-bringing with what I was watching play out in the modern day political arena, I applied to Vander-bilt Divinity School to study theology. There we debated, contemplated and analyzed Scripture (as we say in the South)

"...till the cows came home!"

No sooner did my original *I Didn't Know That* books hit the bookstores, was I met with a new challenge: live audiences bringing in their own stories and questions.

As so many of those early signings were within the reach of my listening audience in Nashville, I no doubt had more than my fair share of questions pertaining to Scripture-related phrases.

With this, I re-opened my books, dusted off my notes, and began refreshing my memory to the many off-handed comments, insights and references I'd picked up along the way.

And with that, I began to make a list...

And that list became this book.

I returned to campus, renewed my library card, and organized a new set of notebooks... The rest, as they say, is history.

My hope is that the words, phrases and stories offered here will inspire you to dust off your own Bible and add to your repertoire of phrases and expressions that come to us straight from the sacred text.

After a whole lot of digging and a whole lot of fun, I'm sufficiently convinced Jesus meant it literally as well as spiritually when he said,

"Seek, and ye shall find."

OLD TESTAMENT

"MADAM, I'M ADAM"

Some say the first words ever spoken were a palindrome. (Big word meaning something that spells the same backwards and forwards.)

Who knows? Maybe God liked name games from the word "Go!" (or in God's case: "Let there be...

light...dark...moon...sun...stars...")
You name it.

Maybe, just maybe, God had a reason for naming things the way he did.

Whether you start with the alphabet, or you start with Genesis, there's no better name than Adam's to get this whole name-game going.

Be it *Adam's apple* or *Adam's rib*, we've tied a lot of labels to the first man ever named, thus expressions were sure to follow.

Today, we *don't know him from Adam*. And according to some, Adam must've had a house cat.

All this becomes more ironic yet when you trace the origin of the first man's name, for Adam is a riddle unto itself.

From the Hebrew word, the name *adam* literally means *human*. The proper name given the first man on earth is a word that appears 225 times in the Old Testament alone.

Adamah (from which it derives) technically means *ground* or *earth*, which provides our first twist, as the name Adam can indicate both one who *works* the ground or one made literally *from* the earth.

Both descriptions tie directly to Adam's role in the beginning. And this naming takes one more twist when, after Adam disobeys God, *adamah* (the ground) is cursed, thus setting the whole story (if not this book) in motion.

Let the name games begin!

In the beginning… could just as easily have read:

    Once a-pun a time…

ADAM'S RIB

(GENESIS 2:22)

Starting with that rib later known as Eve, Genesis 2:22 tells us:

And the rib, which the Lord God had taken
*   from man, made he a woman,*
*   and brought her unto the man.*

What the Scripture does not tell us is how many ribs Adam had before or after he fell into this deep sleep. What's more, no one did a rib count on Eve to compare to see if she came out one extra.

Of interest is that the Hebrew word we translate as "rib" is *tsela*, which, when translated correctly, is not "rib" as is most often thought, but rather "side." By way of interpretation then, some suggest the rib is symbolic of a side-by-side, or a heart-to-heart relationship.

Early Jewish tradition observes that had woman been created from the man's head, she would be superior; had she been created from his feet, she would be subordinate.

That Scripture goes out of its way to say she was created from Adam's rib, well... that paints a picture as more of an equal.

It suggests a side-by-side companion—a best friend... one close to the heart, which lends an even sweeter explanation to a body part too often lost in translation.

ADAM'S APPLE

On the other hand, *Adam's Apple* has nothing to do with Scripture at all, though its origin does link to the man with the same name.

In the mid 1700s, English law forbade surgeons to dissect the human body (with the exception of executed murderers). As a result, cadavers were hard to come by. (For what it's worth, this also gives us such expressions as *skeletons in the closet*, but meanwhile, back to Adam....)

Thanks to William Hunter, a visionary if ever there were one, dissection was introduced to the medical community circa 1747, as Hunter and his students tackled the task of identifying and naming all our internal body parts.

Science was grateful.

But the public was outraged.

But politics aside, it was one innocent little projection in the neck that posed the greatest of all challenges. For this lump kept moving, dodging the surgeon's scalpel, and darting about under the skin.

As legend had long held that this particle was the *forbidden fruit* that got stuck in Adam's throat since the very first sin, Hunter and colleagues let it slide (literally). In efforts to blend science with religion, they named it: *Adam's Apple*—the ultimate truce.

Meanwhile…

DON'T KNOW HIM FROM ADAM

…isn't scriptural either.

Instead, it's a common reference for a person we simply do not know (i.e., a soul we never met).

Given that Adam was created, not born, some (with too much time on their hands) have been known to contemplate his navel. (Since Adam had no birth mother, there would've been no need—for a navel that is, not a mother.)

So technically, we could pick Adam out of a line-up, provided he was wearing no more than a fig leaf. But arguing this point doesn't lend insight to the expression's meaning.

To give credit where credit is due, the phrase in its entirety is:

"Don't know him from Adam's off ox," made popular in the mid 1800s by a book of Nantucket colloquialisms.

Adam's house cat, on the other hand, became the Americanized version of the same expression.

Regardless of the animal you might've tacked on to the end of this one, *don't know him from Adam* is just another way of saying:

"Couldn't pick him out of a crowd of two."

BE FRUITFUL...

*Be fruitful, and multiply, and replenish the earth,
and subdue it: and have dominion over the fish
of the sea, and over the fowl of the air, and over
every living thing that moveth upon the earth.*
(GENESIS 1:28)

An expression not just for rabbits, the command to be fruitful and multiply means exactly what you think: go populate the earth. The phrase is spoken no fewer than six times in the book of Genesis alone, making fruitfulness and multiplication Adam and Eve's number one day job at the opening of the story (Genesis 1:28). Makes sense as someone had to get the human race going.

The next reference is found in Genesis 9:1, when God demands the same of Noah and his sons. (Keep in mind the flood knocked out everyone but those in the ark, leaving only four couples on planet earth to start the population count all over again.)

...AND MULTIPLY

And God blessed Noah and his sons,
and said unto them,
Be fruitful, and multiply, and replenish the earth.
(GENESIS 9:1)

Noah himself may or may not have been much help at this stage, given that he was 600 years old when he came off the boat (Genesis 9:28-29). Thus, it is safe to assume that the brunt of this burden fell upon his three sons: Ham, Shem and Japheth (and, of course, their wives).

No doubt, tackling this fruitful task of repopulating planet earth has its benefits, but when you're starting all over again from ground zero, you do have your work cut out for you.

(Tough job, but someone's got to do it.)

FORBIDDEN FRUIT

Going back to Adam's apple and all things fruitful, truth be told, the Bible doesn't say what fruit it was that was forbidden.

What's more, the Bible never uses the expression *forbidden fruit* as we've come to associate it with anything off limits.

What the Bible does say is this:

And the Lord God commanded the man, saying,
Of every tree of the garden thou mayest freely eat:
But of the tree of the knowledge of good and evil,
thou shalt not eat of it: for in the day
that thou eatest thereof thou shalt surely die.

(*Genesis 2:16-17*)

While your Sunday School flannel boards might've suggested it was an apple, there is really no scriptural reference for this. It's possible that apples just make for ripe visuals. To others it suggests a color synonymous with red hot temptation.

Other scholars trace the apple theory to early Christian Church sources, as the Latin word for apple is *mala*, a word that closely resembled the Latin word *malus* (meaning evil).

WEARING A FIG LEAF

(GENESIS 3:7)

The proverbial fig leaf, wardrobe of choice for naked male statues everywhere, is today synonymous with covering up our more shameful parts. Though when it was popularized in the Renaissance era, fig leaves were merely an artistic attempt at modesty.

Original references trace back to Genesis, however, when from the story of Adam and Eve we are told:

And the eyes of them both were opened,
and they knew that they were naked;
and they sewed fig leaves together,
and made themselves aprons.

(Genesis 3:7)

Fig leaves hit their fashion peak when the Roman Empire converted to Christianity. At this time, heroic nudity all but vanished, relegating art with visibly naked people to depict sinners and the damned.

For what it's worth, the *fig leaf* most often depicted in Roman art is that of an elm or maple, because if you study the actual fig, well... there are gaps in its coverage.

To be fair, the Bible tells us that the attire on which this metaphor was based consisted of many leaves sewn together (as opposed to the one strategic leaf you see on most statues). No doubt when it comes to leaves, size does matter.

(Go fig-ure!)

CURSE OF EVE

Unto the woman he said,
I will greatly multiply thy sorrow and thy conception;
in sorrow thou shalt bring forth children . . .
(GENESIS 3:16)

The curse, as it's referenced today, is a crass term for menstruation, cramps and all things PMS. But while the earliest curse is scriptural, the original wasn't directed to Eve at all, but rather to that tricky serpent that tempted her (who, as far as we know, did not get cramps).

What we do read in Genesis 3:16 is a litany of punishments God bestows upon Eve for eating from the tree she was told to avoid. But technically the curse was placed on the serpent that tempted Eve. Eve's punishment more specifically involved a multiplication of her sorrows.

From the Hebrew word *etsab,* Eve's punishment is labor (both childbirth labor as well physical labor, which is now her lot along with Adam).

Curiously, the King James translates the same word as "sorrow," thus the question becomes: Was Eve's pain physical or was it emotional?

I would surmise there was plenty of both.

Some suggest that Eve's curse goes beyond the physical pain of childbirth and extends to the emotional pain a mother would feel for her children's future (which was clearly uncertain).

To say the least, this would be a postpartum experience of exponential proportion considering that Eve, now banned from her perfect home, would carry the burden of what her actions have now cost her children. By this Eve's curse would extend beyond raw physical pain to encompass the deep remorse a mother might feel in knowing the perfect world she once knew was a place they would never know thanks to her choices.

Pain. Sorrow. The punishment is real. Eve now must work (along with Adam) in order to survive. Life outside of Eden would be no picnic.

One only need factor the birth element alone (pre-epidural) to know that this curse was going to hurt.

SWEAT OF YOUR BROW

(GENESIS 3:19)

A reference to work, the *sweat of your brow* is anything that connotes physical labor.

Specifically, the expression (per the King James) states:

In the sweat of thy face shalt thou eat bread,
till thou return unto the ground;
for out of it wast thou taken:
for dust thou art,
and unto dust shalt thou return.

By way of this story, work became punishment for disobedience, as Adam and Eve must now factor in the day-to-day activities required for their survival.

So was work a paradise before?

This remains a puzzle. But we do know Adam had tasks to do already. Specifically, he was put in the garden to dress and keep it (Genesis 2:15), but then there was that whole populating the planet part that not everybody calls work.

But this we do know: once they sinned, life changed dramatically for Adam and Eve.

Their routines of walking and talking with God are now replaced by physical labor and all things painful.

Not only will they struggle *by the sweat of their brows*, they are likewise destined to return to the dust from which they were created, which suggests life got a lot more stressful (if not more mortal) than originally intended.

ORIGINAL SIN

Stemming from man's fall from grace, the concept of *original sin* came into being as a result of Adam and Eve's decision to eat the forbidden fruit. But to be clear, the phrase itself is nowhere found in the Bible.

Given that in their original state, Adam and Eve were innocent beings, their transgression (by way of their choice to go for the fruit of the tree) extends to the whole of humanity.

By this, *original sin* (also called "hereditary sin" or "birth sin") suggests that sin is now in our genetic make-up, and that all humans from this point on will be born sinners and will die sinners without some form of intervention.

To correct this separation between God and God's created, the early Church incorporated the "born again" ritual of baptism to cancel all sin (original or otherwise).

The concept made for lively theological debate especially around the time of Augustine (354-430 A.D.) as the question became, "What happens to those innocent infants who die before they are old enough to be baptized?"

Of this was born the ritual of infant baptism or "sprinkling," still common in certain Catholic, Methodist, Presbyterian and Episcopal churches today.

FALL OF MAN

And speaking of phrases not found in the Bible, *fall of man*, (also known as "the fall") is right up there with the notion of *original sin*.

As a matter of doctrine, the premise is this: Thanks to Adam and Eve's eating the forbidden fruit from the Tree of Knowledge of Good and Evil, mankind and the whole of creation from this point forward has fallen from grace.

True, the original theory traces to Genesis, but the actual words aren't found there. Rather, the label is one of theological creation, summing up the scenario after Adam and Eve are cast out of the garden of Eden.

As the couple fell from their original state of purity and innocence, their disobedience causes the whole of mankind to suffer in sin forever. (Or, as Christians believe... until Jesus died for sins.)

There are other immediate ramifications thanks to this momentous occasion.

For instance:

Serpents get to belly-crawl.

Women get painful labor (not to mention they get to answer to their husbands for the rest of their lives, as if labor wasn't painful enough).

And, men will forever struggle with crops from land once receptive.

But the greatest tragedy of *the fall* is that this is the event that first introduces the spiritual separation of creation (humankind) from creator (God).

Beyond these specifics, the fall of man is the result of poor choices made by our first human ambassadors—those who just could not resist that forbidden fruit from the Tree of the Knowledge of Good and Evil.

ASHES TO ASHES...

From the scriptural reference in Genesis 3:19 we read:

In the sweat of thy face shalt thou eat bread,
till thou return unto the ground;
for out of it wast thou taken:
for dust thou art,
and unto dust shalt thou return.

The dust part we have figured out. We humans are made of earthly elements, so dust bunnies we are destined to be.

But when called on the carpet after breaking God's commandment (the one about eating from the Tree of Knowledge), Adam and Eve get the first glimpse of their future by way of the part that reads:

...dust thou art, and unto dust shalt thou return.

DUST TO DUST

Dust to dust in this context refers to man's mortality—the ultimate punishment for lives now filled with human struggles and pain.

First, hard work, then agonizing pain, and ultimately death are the consequences of disobedience.

As for *ashes to ashes*, well, that part's not scriptural. Instead it comes from the Book of Common Prayer, added for recitation at Anglican burial services.

To be clear, the phrase most commonly referenced is:

Earth to earth, ashes to ashes… dust to dust;
in sure and certain hope of the Resurrection
into eternal life.

RAISING CAIN

(GENESIS 4)

A modern colloquialism stemming from the Biblical story of Cain, the phrase *Raising Cain* suggests a ruckus or a great disturbance. We've Americanized it in some parts of the country with the phrase: *to raise the devil*.

Raising Cain, however, hearkens to the Genesis 4 account of Cain (son of Adam and Eve) whose vegetarian offering was rejected by God in favor of his brother's animal sacrifice. The plot thickens when jealousy (we assume) overtakes, moving Cain to kill his brother, Abel. As punishment, God curses the ground from which Cain (the farmer) would work, and curses Cain as well, exiling him to a life of wandering.

For what it's worth, the phrase *Raising Cain* is not found in the Bible, but instead traces to the "St. Louis Pennant" where it first appeared in an 1840s comic strip.

Less a commentary on child rearing, more a figure of speech on trouble-making, *Raising Cain* finds its roots in Scripture, but certainly not its wording.

And the Lord said unto Cain, Why art thou wroth? and why is thy countenance fallen?

If thou doest well, shalt thou not be accepted? and if thou doest not well, sin lieth at the door. And unto thee shall be his desire, and thou shalt rule over him.

And Cain talked with Abel his brother: and it came to pass, when they were in the field, that Cain rose up against Abel his brother, and slew him.

And the Lord said unto Cain, Where is Abel thy brother? And he said, I know not: Am I my brother's keeper?

And he said, What hast thou done? the voice of thy brother's blood crieth unto me from the ground.

And now art thou cursed from the earth....

(Genesis 4:6-11)

"AM I MY BROTHER'S KEEPER?"

(GENESIS 4:9-16)

So if asked in a trivia game, the line belongs to Cain, firstborn of Adam and Eve... the Bible's first recorded murderer.

The plot is this: Cain kills Abel. (Most assume out of jealousy.) God comes knocking and asks, *"Where is Abel, thy brother?"*

Cain replies *"I know not."* (Even though he does. He's just not saying.) Next... the infamous line, *"Am I my brother's keeper?"*

From here, curses abound. Cain is cursed. The ground from which Cain derived his livelihood is cursed (which for a farmer is a double curse). And the Bible goes on to tell us:

...Cain went out from the presence of the Lord, and dwelt in the land of Nod, east of Eden.

(A whole new trivia category, in case you want to brush up on your literary classics—I'm thinking of John Steinbeck, in particular.)

Meanwhile, though cursed, Cain is still God's own—protected from harm by way of a mark, which also gives you another classic: *the mark of Cain.*

And the Lord said unto Cain, Where is Abel thy brother? And he said, I know not: Am I my brother's keeper?

And he said, What hast thou done? the voice of thy brother's blood crieth unto me from the ground.

And now art thou cursed from the earth, which hath opened her mouth to receive thy brother's blood from thy hand...

(Genesis 4:9-11)

LAND OF NOD

(GENESIS 4:16)

A place for drifters, this land of Nod is both a mythical place as well as a geographical one according to the book of Genesis.

Originally, Nod is that land east of Eden, best known for being Cain's place of exile after he murdered his brother, Abel.

Scripture tells us:

And Cain went out from the presence of the Lord, and dwelt in the land of Nod on the east of Eden...

(Genesis 4:16)

By way of Hebrew interpretation, this land was aptly named, as Nod is the Hebrew word for wanderer.

Of other Biblical significance, Nod is also noted as the place where Enoch, Cain's oldest, was born—the son for whom the Bible's first city was named, as we're told in Genesis 4:17.

Unless you're a Bible aficionado, you might not have associated Nod with a town or a place but rather a state of being, as in nodding off to sleep, which likewise involves a bit of drifting.

Nod's modern-day association with a state of sleeping can be credited to Jonathan Swift, who first referenced the word in his *Complete Collection of Polite and Ingenious Conversation* in 1737. But we can also thank Robert Louis Stevenson who, more than a century later, poetically turned the phrase when he penned the words:

> *From breakfast on through all the day*
> *At home among my friends I stay,*
> *But every night I go abroad*
> *Afar into the land of Nod.*

From A Child's Garden of Verses and Underwoods (1885)

OLD AS METHUSELAH

*And all the days of Methuselah were
nine hundred sixty and nine years: and he died.*
(GENESIS 5:27)

In case you didn't know... Methuselah was Noah's grandpa, and is believed by some to be oldest man in recorded history.

The Genesis account tells us that Methuselah lived to be 969 years old. But more impressive than this, he was fathering sons (namely Noah's father, Lamech) when he was 187 years old!

As a result, Methuselah has become the proverbial symbol of longevity.

Old as Methuselah (the expression) traces back as far as the 14th century, which makes the phrase itself almost as old as the man.

Ironically, when compared to other Ancient Near Eastern writings that reference antediluvian kings ("antediluvian" being a fancy word for "pre-flood" in case you were about to look it up), there were others we are told who likewise lived for thousands of years, which means by some standards of record-keeping, Methuselah was downright young.

No way to know for sure how years were counted back then. But given that Genesis goes to great length to factor the ages into Noah's genealogy, it's interesting to put a pencil to the math, as Methuselah would have still been alive as Noah was boarding the animals onto the ark.

Sadly (if not ironically) he dies the year the flooding begins.

(No way to know if he refused to get on board or if the stress of just watching his grandson finally did him in.)

BOW IN THE CLOUDS

I do set my bow in the cloud, and it shall be
for a token of a covenant between me and the earth.
(GENESIS 9:13-16)

Most folks hear the words "bow" and "clouds" in the same sentence and conclude: Oh. Rainbow! But it is of significance to note that the word we translate as such comes from the Hebrew word *qeshet*, which interpreted, can mean either a rainbow or an archer's bow.

The latter is an instrument of war, which some scholars construe as divine wrath. (Think arrows for thunderbolts shooting from the heavens at an enemy down below… in this case, all of mankind.)

Ancient art reinforces this notion with its various deities wielding such bows, with the laying down of a bow symbolizing an end to battle.

(SOME CALL IT A RAINBOW!)

But bows carry another meaning. The story of Noah tells us that the Lord was at war with man (if not himself for creating man), saddened that his perfect creation was now "...*filled with violence*" (Genesis 6:13).

In Biblical terms, bows carry an archer's symbolism, representing military strength, power to take over... power to destroy.

In a more peaceful context, the bow (whether in the sky or on its side) would represent a new commitment of understanding.

Either way, God's power, as well as God's promise of peace, culminates in one common symbol: a *bow in the clouds*, which (in this story) also marked the end of the flood.

PROMISED LAND

Also known as Canaan, Canaan's Land, and the Land of Milk and Honey, the Promised Land was that land promised by God to Abraham, Isaac, Jacob, and later to Moses on behalf of the children of Israel.

Otherwise known as the Land of Israel, the Promised Land is that land promised to belong forever to God's chosen people.

To Abraham it was promised:

Unto thy seed have I given this land, from the river of Egypt, unto the great river, the river Euphrates. (Genesis 15:18)

To his son Isaac it was promised:

For unto thee, and unto thy seed, I will give all these countries… (Genesis 26:3)

To Isaac's son, Jacob, it was promised:

The land whereon thou liest, to thee will I give it, and to thy seed... (Genesis 28:13)

And when the children of Israel were freed by Moses, the Promised Land is key again, as Scripture tells us:

And Moses went up from the plains of Moab unto the mountain of Nebo... and the Lord shewed him all the land of Gilead... (Deuteronomy 34:1)

From this view, the Lord tells Moses:

This is the land which I sware unto Abraham, unto Isaac, and unto Jacob... I will give it unto thy seed... Just before the ominous prediction: *I have caused thee to see it with thine eyes, but thou shalt not go over thither. (Deuteronomy 34:4)*

It was Joshua who first stepped foot in the Promised Land (after the death of Moses). Joshua 1:1-6 describes this long awaited moment.

MESS O' POTTAGE

(GENESIS 25:29-34)

An expression synonymous with something of little to no value, otherwise exchanged for something very important, the first *mess o' pottage* traces to the story of Jacob and Esau (Isaac's twin boys and grandsons of Abraham. You with me here? Because this story just keeps getting better and better).

When Jacob, the younger twin, sets his sights to claim the inheritance due firstborns, he schemes with his mother to trick his aging father into blessing him with the rights that were supposed to go to Esau.

Enter Esau (the older of the twins), exhausted from a long day of hunting. Upon hitting the doorway he is met with the savory smells of a home-cooked meal. (The Bible calls it pottage; we would call it lentil soup.)

Exhausted and mindless, Esau gives up his birthright in exchange for a hot meal, falling prey to the cunning of Jacob's ploy.

As a result, *mess o' pottage* is today credited as one of the most significant inheritance deals in recorded history, as Jacob (later renamed Israel) goes on to father a nation, which in turn becomes God's chosen people.

And Jacob sod pottage: and Esau came from the field, and he was faint: And Esau said to Jacob, Feed me, I pray thee, with that same red pottage; for I am faint: therefore was his name called Edom. And Jacob said, Sell me this day thy birthright. And Esau said, Behold, I am at the point to die: and what profit shall this birthright do to me? And Jacob said, Swear to me this day; and he sware unto him: and he sold his birthright unto Jacob. Then Jacob gave Esau bread and pottage of lentiles; and he did eat and drink, and rose up, and went his way: thus Esau despised his birthright.

(Genesis 25:29-34)

STONE PILLOW

(GENESIS 28:10-22)

So as you might imagine, once that whole *mess o' pottage* scheme was hatched, Jacob wasn't exactly winning points with his brother or his father. As a result, his mother, Rebeka, helps him escape to his Uncle Laban's to live until the family storm subsides. It is here he will meet his future bride(s), father twelve sons (not all at once), and become the head of a brand new nation (namely: Israel).

Somewhere between Beer-sheba and Haran, we are told Jacob lies down for the night, placing his head on a pillow of stone. (Not the most comfortable of head rests if you ask me, but given all the trouble he was in, I'm sure he fell asleep the minute his head hit the pillow and no doubt, slept like a rock!)

When he awakes from his dream, Jacob (affected by its imagery) proclaims, *"God is truly in this place,"* and he proceeds to make an altar of his pillow. Anointing it with oil he names the place *Beth El* (Hebrew for House of God).

And he lighted upon a certain place, and tarried there all night, because the sun was set; and he took of the stones of that place, and put them for his pillows, and lay down in that place to sleep.

And he dreamed, and behold a ladder set up on the earth, and the top of it reached to heaven: and behold the angels of God ascending and descending on it.

And Jacob awaked out of his sleep, and he said, Surely the Lord is in this place; and I knew it not.

(Genesis 28:11-12, 16)

JACOB'S LADDER

(GENESIS 28:13-17)

Meanwhile, regarding this dream that Jacob had while sleeping on this *pillow of stone*, it involves a ladder reaching into heaven. With angels ascending and angels descending, he hears the voice of God say,

> … *I am the LORD God of Abraham thy father,*
> *and the God of Isaac: the land whereon thou liest,*
> *to thee will I give it, and to thy seed*
> *…in thee and in thy seed shall*
> *all the families of the earth be blessed.*
>
> *(Genesis 28:13-14)*

Upon waking, Jacob concludes he has literally been in the presence of God, and in awestruck fear declares this place to be

> …*the gate of heaven.*

From this, the pillar is anointed and named Beth El—memorializing the place where Jacob first vows to make the Lord his God. (Keep in mind that Jacob is soon to be re-named Israel, father of the Children of Israel, otherwise known as God's chosen.)

In addition to the promises made in this dream, Scripture offers some of the most comforting words a person could hear, when the Lord says to Jacob:

And, behold, I am with thee,
and will keep thee in all places whither thou goest,
and will bring thee again into this land;
for I will not leave thee, until I have done
that which I have spoken to thee of.

(Genesis 28:15)

COAT OF MANY COLORS

(GENESIS 37:3)

Not to be confused with that folksy Dolly Parton tune, the biblical coat of many colors is the one Jacob gives to Joseph in a move that triggered a chain reaction even Andrew Lloyd Webber would come to honor (via "Joseph and the Amazing Technicolor Dreamcoat").

Now to be clear, the Hebrew phrase *kethonet passim* means "long coat with stripes." The "many colors" came later, derived from the Septuagint (i.e., the Greek version of the Hebrew Bible), which in turn made its way into the King James Bible most of us grew up on.

Whether colored, striped or both, what we do know is that this was a coat of great contention within the family:

Now Israel loved Joseph more than all his children, because he was the son of his old age: and he made him a coat of many colours.

(Genesis 37:3)

Genesis makes no bones about the fact that Joseph was Jacob's favorite, but in bestowing such a gift, implications were that the younger would usurp the eldest, thus bucking the lineage of family succession.

Tensions mount when Joseph shares his dreams of his brothers bowing down to him.

(O.K. Maybe not his smartest move.)

The combination of these events sparks a fraternal coup, wherein the brothers team up against Joseph and sell him as a slave to Ishmaelite merchants for 20 pieces of silver.

At this point Joseph's coat takes on real color, as the brothers dip it in goat blood and return it to their father, saying Joseph was savaged by wild beasts.

Fortunately, while the brothers did get his goat (and his coat), the story has a happy ending. Keep reading!

LAND O' GOSHEN

(GENESIS 45:10)

In Southern vernacular, *Land o' Goshen* is right up there with Heaven's to Betsy. But unlike Betsy's heaven, *Land o' Goshen* was a very real place.

Located in the northeast part of the Nile Delta, the moisture of these green pastures made for lush, plush and particularly desirable grazing lands for sheep and cattle.

This same land was offered by Joseph (now rubbing elbows with Pharaoh) as the new home for his brothers and his father (two years into Egypt's seven-year famine—a famine predicted in Pharaoh's dream of fat and skinny cows).

In short, *Land o' Goshen* was some of Egypt's finest turf...

Specifically, we're told:

And thou shalt dwell in the Land of Goshen, and thou shalt be near unto me, thou, and thy children, and thy children's children, and thy flocks, and thy herds, and all thou hast...

The reference comes after Joseph (of coat of many colors fame) was sold by his jealous brothers into slavery. When a turn of events puts Joseph in charge, just as his brothers come in search of food, they discover all too soon that their brother is alive and well (and quite powerful at this stage of things).

With five more years of famine still on the horizon, Joseph implores his brothers to bring his father (Jacob) and move to the *Land of Goshen...* a windfall of a gift in light of the cruel manner in which they had treated him earlier.

Today the expression is much akin to *"Goodness sakes!"*—signifying a pleasant outcome, from the last place (or person) you'd expect.

LIVING OFF THE FAT
OF THE LAND

(GENESIS 45:17-18)

In its original context, *living off the fat of the land* suggests just that: living off the bounty of Mother Earth herself (with "fat" being a reference to the richness of the harvest, not that necessarily of cow's milk). But the more modern use of the expression suggests life lived in great affluence, often to excess and without necessarily having earned it. In this latter context, the phrase carries a negative connotation, suggesting that such a life has come just a little too easy, either by entitlement or non-deserving means.

If we trace this phrase to Scripture we can see where both meanings might apply, as Genesis describes quite literally a gift of great value, bestowed upon the family of Joseph (yes, the one with the Technicolor Dreamcoat, compliments of Pharaoh).

According to Scripture:

Pharaoh said unto Joseph, Say unto thy brethren, this do ye: lade your beasts, and go, get you unto the land of Canaan; And take your father and your households and come unto me: and I will give you the good of the land of Egypt, and ye shall eat the fat of the land.

(Genesis 45:17-18)

Recalling our Old Testament patriarchs, Joseph, the eleventh and favored son of Jacob (whose name later became Israel), was sold by his jealous brothers into slavery, but through a series of divine appointments, he rose to become the second most powerful man in all of Egypt (second only to Pharaoh himself).

When these same brothers came to Egypt several years later, mid famine, in search of food, Joseph shows compassion to his kin and offers forgiveness while Pharaoh gifts Joseph's family with one prime piece of real estate—also known as the Land of Goshen.

BURNING BUSH

(EXODUS 3:2-4)

The compactus plant notwithstanding (fancy name for that fiery red bush we Southerners stick in our flower beds to add color in the off seasons), the original burning bush was more dramatic yet.

Its story is found in Exodus. Its symbolism marks the beginning of Moses' interaction with God that sets the stage for the birth of the Israelite nation.

Found on Mount Horeb (also known as Sinai), the bush is described in Scripture as engulfed by flames, though never consumed. (But wait! That's only half the miracle.)

In addition to not combusting as it burns, this plant talks! And not just any talk mind you, this message was direct from God.

When instructed to take off his sandals (for he is standing on holy ground), Moses converses with God and is told he will be the one to lead the children of Israel out of Egypt and into Canaan (i.e., the Promised Land).

From the Hebrew word *seneh* (which sounds like Sinai—the famous mount upon which Moses received the Ten Commandments), the *burning bush* is today's eternal metaphor for all things epiphany—big word meaning a manifestation or appearance of the divine, such as that which Moses experienced when talking directly with God.

Meanwhile fire (which is used throughout Scripture) is forevermore linked to divine appearances. (Think pillar of fire that led the children of Israel; think flaming tongues, referenced in Acts, representing the Holy Spirit in the New Testament.)

A sure (fire) way to grab your attention, for sure—a talking, burning bush is all but guaranteed to have you take off your shoes and sit for a spell.

MANNA FROM HEAVEN

(EXODUS 16:15)

An expression that signifies a miracle sent from on high, the original manna from heaven was precisely that—a miracle that fell from the sky (quite literally).

The setting: the children of Israel, former slaves, but following the Exodus from Egypt— no longer under Pharaoh's rule, have been led by their leader, Moses, through the Red Sea and into the wilderness, to begin their lives in freedom as God's chosen people.

The challenge: These newly released slaves, far from familiar with what freedom entails, soon become disgruntled and fearful. They begin to wonder if they should have perhaps remained in slavery where at least they could count on being fed. They yearn for the "flesh pots" of Egypt (Exodus 16:3), which refers not to houses of prostitution, but to kettles with meat.

Moses instructs this group of former slaves that God would provide, and provide God did, with quail in the evening for meat and manna each morning for bread. The Israelites were told to gather only enough manna for a day's supply of food, but to collect two days' worth on Friday, as there was to be no work on the Sabbath.

As we might imagine, some just had to test the theory, and in so doing, watched their hoarded supply of manna become useless and bug-infested grain—thus Scripture reinforces the notion that God alone provides.

And when the children of Israel saw it, they said one to another, It is manna: for they wist not what it was. And Moses said unto them, This is the bread which the LORD hath given you to eat.

(Exodus 16:15)

EYE FOR AN EYE

(EXODUS 21:23-27)

The concept of *an eye for an eye* is Biblical in nature, legal in translation, and quite simple in meaning.

Today, we'd call it: tit for tat.

Under Mosaic law, anyone who took the eye of another (intentionally or by accident) would face equal punishment. (In other words, prepare to lose an eye of your own!)

The concept was one of equal retribution. Scholars believe it was designed to keep the level of punishment to a minimum, allowing retribution to equal only that of the precise crime and no more.

A principle noted throughout the Old Testament, you might recall that Jesus overturned this notion in his Sermon on the Mount when (citing the original), he adds a new, more compassionate addendum...

TOOTH FOR A TOOTH

You have heard that it hath been said,
An eye for an eye, and a tooth for a tooth:
But I say unto you, That ye resist not evil:
but whosoever shall smite thee on thy right cheek,
turn to him the other also.
(MATTHEW 5:38-39)

Keep in mind, the principle applied to more than just eyes and teeth. In its original form, any body part could be substituted (eye for an eye; tooth for a tooth, a hand for a hand, a foot for a foot).

While most credit Moses as being the originator of the whole eye for an eye concept, other scholars credit the Code of Hammaurabi (one of the earliest and best preserved sets of laws known to man), which traces back to ancient Babylon (circa 1760 B.C.).

GOLDEN CALF

(EXODUS 32:4-35)

A problematic idol born of impatient children (namely the children of Israel) while waiting on Moses to come down from the mountain, the story of this image is significant for a number of reasons.

Keep in mind it was Aaron (brother of Moses) who gave in to the masses, crafting the *golden calf* that would forever be captured in our language.

In their defense, it wasn't uncommon to worship the bovine, as bulls were fairly common deities throughout the Ancient Near East. But when the children of Israel began giving all credit to an inanimate object (after all God had done to bring them out of their slavery), well... to say Moses was angry would be an understatement.

He smashed the two tablets to the ground. Apparently even the greatest of leaders can throw a temper tantrum.

But more curious yet is the ending of this story, for according to Scripture, Moses

...took the calf which they had made, and burnt it in the fire, and ground it to powder, and strawed it upon the water, and made the children of Israel drink of it.

(Exodus 32:20)

On the one hand, it was quite the dyspeptic burial, but on the other, it did get results.

Still, some ponder the scene, noting the heat it would take to turn a statue of gold into dust-like powder (considering the limited resources available in the middle of the desert).

Regardless, the story can't help but leave you marveling at the mystery (if not the intensity) of God's "no bull" policy.

"I'VE BEEN TO THE MOUNTAINTOP"

(FROM THE SPEECH OF
MARTIN LUTHER KING, JR.)

We've got some difficult days ahead. But it doesn't matter with me now…

Because I've been to the mountaintop… and I've seen the Promised Land.

I may not get there with you. But I want you to know tonight, that we, as a people, will get to the Promised Land.

To be clear, these words as spoken here are not the Bible. It's his reference to seeing the Promised Land that grips us given the events that follow Rev. Martin Luther King's impassioned speech on civil rights.

The mountaintop referred to here is none other than Mt. Nebo, mountaintop from which Moses catches his first glimpse of his own Promised Land.

Like the Reverend King, Moses could *see* the Promised Land, he *spoke* of the Promised Land, he *dreamt* of the Promised Land. But sadly, neither man lived to experience the Promised Land.

Just to remind, the Promised Land was (scripturally speaking) that land promised to the children of Israel (i.e., the descendants of Abraham, Isaac and Jacob).

It was also known as:

—the Land of Canaan

—the Land of Milk and Honey

—Canaan's Land or simply (for those who actually made it there)—Canaan.

As it pertains to Dr. King's reference in his famous speech given the night before his assassination, the Promised Land is forever metaphorical for all things peaceful and harmonious.

The picture was that of a time when all people, regardless of race, regardless of color, would live together as equals under the law.

MAN DOES NOT LIVE BY BREAD ALONE

And he humbled thee, and suffered thee to hunger,
and fed thee with manna, which thou knewest not,
neither did thy fathers know; that he might make thee
know that man doth not live by bread only,
but by every word that proceedeth out of
the mouth of the LORD doth man live.
(DEUTERONOMY 8:3)

The first recording of this oft-quoted phrase is found in the Old Testament book of Deuteronomy. Moses teaches that the children of Israel, tested in the wilderness and experiencing the manna God miraculously provided them, have to learn that life is not simply determined by what one eats, even if that food is divinely provided. It is God who provided everything the children of Israel needed to live. More important than the manna itself was God's instruction that accompanied it, which was that they "forget not the Lord" and follow his "commandments, his ordinances and his statues." (Deuteronomy 8:11)

Today, the phrase "Man does not live by bread alone" has become synonymous with the human soul's need for meaning and spiritual fulfillment... aspects of living that go far beyond the physical.

American psychologist Abraham Maslow (1908-1970) suggested a similar notion with his "hierarchy of needs"; Dr. Maslow proposed that while living beings require the basics of food, shelter and clothing, more evolved beings require fulfillment, meaning and experiences of spiritual significance.

Man cannot live by bread alone can be found in both the Old and New Testaments. Scripture tells us Satan attempted to entice Jesus, after his 40-day fast, to turn stones into bread in order to avoid starving. But rather than yield to temptations, Jesus cites this Old Testament Scripture, reminding us again that life is more than a body, and our needs, more than physical.

APPLE OF MY EYE

(DEUTERONOMY 32:10)

So if you're asking, "What's with the apple and who's eye was it?" you will here and forevermore be in the know.

Apple of my eye references one held dear. The object of this great affection would (by definition) be the pride of the family.

In scriptural context, this baby would be God's own (i.e., the children of Israel).

The eye? That would be God's eye, ever watching over His own. The Song of Moses states,

He found him in a desert land, and in the waste howling wilderness; he led him about, he instructed him, he kept him as the apple of his eye.

(*Deuteronomy 32:10*)

A metaphor referenced no fewer than five times as the nation of Israel evolves, it's no wonder we all know the expression.

Repetition alone suggests that when it comes to these children of Israel, they are... well, special —if not downright chosen! Their father (God) loves them so much.

In the book of Psalms David appeals to God, begging:

Keep me as the apple of the eye, hide me under the shadow of thy wings.

(Psalm 17:8)

In Proverbs 7:2, Solomon likewise makes reference to the apple:

Keep my commandments, and live; and my law as the apple of thine eye.

There are two other references to this favored status: one in Lamentations; another in Zechariah. But the bottom line is... God's children (of Israel) are the original

Apple of God's Eye!

HITTING THE NAIL ON THE HEAD

(JUDGES 4:17-21)

To nail something means you expose it for truth. It's an expression some trace to merchants who nailed bogus money to their shop doors as fair warning to anyone that might consider the notion of counterfeiting.

But *hit the nail on the head* and you are in for a Bible story that once took the phrase to heart.

To be fair, this phrase is not found verbatim in Scripture, but the expression takes on Biblical significance when you make reference to *hitting the nail on head*.

Undeniably one of the best (albeit gruesome) stories to come out of the Old Testament... from the book of Judges comes a woman named Jael who took the expression, well... quite literally.

An assassination predicted by the prophetess Deborah, the story is a colorful one (but I warn you—it's bloody).

When Sisera (Israel's enemy) flees the battle-field on foot seeking shelter from God's chosen, he thinks he's found comfort in the tent of Jael (whom he thought was his ally).

We are told Jael took him into her tent, gave him milk, and covered him with a blanket.

But as he slept, the Bible says Jael (wife of Heber), with hammer in hand,

...went softly unto him, and smote the nail into his temples and fastened it into the ground: for he was fast asleep and weary. So he died.

(Judges 4:21)

A rather gruesome ending, but it did net Israel forty more years of peace. For my money this one takes the cake for the most graphic depiction of a phrase with Biblical ties.

BRINGING DOWN THE HOUSE

(JUDGES 16:25-30)

Most often used in theatrical context, *bringing down the house* suggests a performance so good that the theatre vibrates to the point of collapse, owing to the thunderous applause.

Sadly, such was not case in the Bible's own version of the phrase. The first house brought down was that of the Philistine lords, who had gathered to celebrate the capture of the Bible's strongest man (namely, Samson).

Seduced into shaving his hair (source of his strength), Samson lost all power when Delilah, the woman with whom he was smitten, did him in.

Little did Samson know, Delilah worked for the enemy (i.e., the Philistines), who in turn shackled him and gouged out his eyes.

But while his strength left him, the Lord never did, and in a final act of vengeance, Samson (in his farewell performance) asked his captors to lead him to the pillars upon which their (Philistine) temple rested.

While his captors partied on in celebration and mockery, Samson prayed to God for one final act of strength, and literally *bringing down the house*, killed everyone inside.

And Samson took hold of the two middle pillars upon which the house stood, and on which it was borne up, of the one with his right hand, and of the other with his left.

And Samson said, Let me die with the Philistines. And he bowed himself with all his might; and the house fell upon the lords, and upon all the people that were therein. So the dead which he slew at his death were more than they which he slew in his life.

(Judges 16:29-30)

MAN AFTER MY OWN HEART

But now thy kingdom shall not continue:
the Lord hath sought him a man after his own heart,
and the Lord hath commanded him to be
captain over his people, because thou hast not kept
that which the Lord commanded thee.
(I SAMUEL 13:14)

An expression most use to suggest a person of kindred spirit, the first *Man After My Own Heart* is found in the book of Samuel (later in the book of Acts) and speaks to a love so deep that hearts are identical.

But no matter which half of the Bible you come from, the phrase *Man After My Own Heart* is first recorded in the Old Testament book of 1 Samuel and refers to God's love, in this case, for David. Thanks to the books bearing his name, Samuel (the prophet who anointed Israel's first two kings) writes at length of David—a man laden with human frailties, and yet known for loving God and forever seeking God's will in his life.

Keep in mind it was Samuel (child apprentice to Eli, the priest) who heard God call him by name and answered saying:

Speak: for thy servant heareth.

(I Samuel 3:4)

That the Lord sought *a man after his own heart* suggests that God was looking for leaders of his own choosing (as opposed to a kingship built on royal bloodlines, in which case Saul's sons would have succeeded him).

When King Saul deviates from God's instruction, it is Samuel who prophesies that Saul's kingdom will not last, and later Samuel (from the grave) who predicts Saul's death.

From this, an expression synonymous with all things faithful, suggests it is loyalty, not lineage, that determines one's worth in God's eyes.

SPLITTING THE BABY

(I KINGS 3:15-28)

A common expression referenced in custody cases even today, the very image of *splitting the baby* suggests a difficult decision wherein fleshing out the truth is the only hope for cure.

The original baby-splitting scenario takes place when King Solomon (known for his wisdom) is faced with the difficult task of determining between two women (each claiming to be the mother of the same baby) just which is the real mother.

When one woman smothers her own child in her sleep, she swaps her (dead) child with the living child of another, leaving it to Solomon to decide which mother is for real.

Once he hears both sides, Solomon rules that the baby must be split (his test to determine the real mother by way of her maternal instincts).

When the mother of the dead child agrees, the true mother's identity is revealed.

With maternal instinct kicking in she asks Solomon to let the child live, even if it has to be with the false mother.

With this, the verdict is clear as Solomon wisely discerns which woman is telling the truth, and he returns the baby to its rightful mother.

And the king said, Divide the living child in two, and give half to the one, and half to the other.

Then spake the woman whose the living child was unto the king, for her bowels yearned upon her son, and she said, O my lord, give her the living child, and in no wise slay it. But the other said, Let it be neither mine nor thine, but divide it.

Then the king answered and said, Give her the living child, and in no wise slay it: she is the mother thereof.

(I Kings 3:25-27)

SWING LOW, SWEET CHARIOT

(II KINGS 2:11-12)

Swing Low, Sweet Chariot,
Coming for to carry me home.
Swing Low, Sweet Chariot,
Coming for to carry me home.
I looked over Jordon and what did I see?
Coming for to carry me home…
A band of angels, coming after me.
Coming for to carry me home…

Composed in 1862 by a slave named Wallis Willis, this African-American spiritual was said to have been inspired by a river in Arkansas that reminded Wallis of the River Jordan where Jesus was baptized.

The scriptural basis for the song comes from the story of Elijah, the prophet, who was taken up to heaven in a chariot of fire.

As he talks with Elisha (his soon-to-be successor), the Bible tells us:

And it came to pass, as they still went on, and talked, that, behold, there appeared a chariot of fire, and horses of fire, and parted them both asunder; and Elijah went up by a whirlwind into heaven.

(II Kings 2:11)

It would have been a powerfully emotional scene to watch your beloved whisked into the clouds by a fiery chariot. This was an event foreshadowing Jesus' own ascension according to some scholars (though in Jesus' version there are no chariots of fire, only clouds).

PAINTED JEZEBEL

(II KINGS 9:30-37)

You can call her Jezzi or you can call her Belle, but either way, this Jezebel woman (also known as Painted Jezebel) was one made up lady! A Phoenician princess who marries King Ahab (king of Israel's Northern Kingdom), Jezebel is best known for:

a) enticing her husband to worship Baal (which in turn, lures those children of Israel right back into their idol-worshipping ways),

b) killing off Israel's prophets, and

c) wearing really heavy make up.

Her name would become synonymous with shameless women everywhere, and her story boasts a plot line thicker than her eyeliner and twice as dramatic.

To top it off, her demise was downright ominous, made more eerie yet by way of its prediction by Elijah the prophet.

And what a demise it was!

For starters, Jezebel's violent death (foretold by the prophet Elijah in I Kings 21:23) is graphically depicted in Scripture right down to the wild dogs that consumed her body after she fell from her upstairs window.

(O.K. It was really more like a *push*.)

We're told there was nothing left of her, save for her skull, her feet and the palms of her hands (which, not making for great dog food, were left behind in the street below).

A name since equated with hussies, prostitutes and all things slutty, it is thanks to the book of Revelation (2:20) that her name is stigmatized forever. (Ironically, Jezebel—while yes, a liar and a murderer—was actually a faithful wife. Mean, yes. But loyal to her causes, which sadly included idols, netting her the bad rep she still carries today.)

OLD AS THE HILLS

(JOB 15:7)

A countrified expression for one who is very, very old, *Old as the Hills* is a country favorite.

Some might toss it right up there with such classics as *Older than God's Dog*, but that would be mixing your metaphors, as God's dog is not mentioned in the Bible, but *Old as the Hills* is both traceable and scriptural!

The expression traces to Job, who has gone through a series of hard knocks. In processing his plight with friends, Job ponders the nature of God, debating whether God's relationship to mankind is one of benevolent intercessor or indifferent creator.

In a series of philosophical questions that would make Socrates proud, Job poses a number of theological theories as he works to make sense of his otherwise undeserved suffering (the scriptural equivalent of *When Bad Things Happen to Good People*).

Old as the Hills is first used by Job's friend Eliphaz in efforts to convince Job that his suffering is not without meaning.

Eliphaz suggests that God's wisdom is greater than Job's comprehension when he poses the phrase as a rhetorical question (big word meaning we know the answer before we ask it). He asks:

> *Art thou the first man that was born?*
> *Or wast thou made before the hills?*

(Job 15:7)

95

NOTHING BUT
SKIN AND BONES

(JOB 19:20)

An expression still cited in pop culture today, a person said to be *nothing but skin and bones* is most often some sickly creature (if not another Hollywood starlet turned anorexic).

First appearing in the Geneva Bible in 1560, *skin and bones* was a part of Job's reply to Bildad when discussing his miserable plight. After being stripped of his worldly goods, his family, and his health, the only thing left is life itself (which he's barely hanging onto at that). Still and so it is in this that we gained our expression. Picked up by the King James, the phrase reads:

My bone cleaveth to my skin and to my flesh, and I am escaped with the skin of my teeth.

Which leads us to another classic...

BY THE SKIN OF MY TEETH

(JOB 19:20)

To be sure, teeth don't have skin, though some scholars have suggested the reference was to that teeny, tiny, thin layer of porcelain-like enamel that tops our teeth (which would no doubt, be very thin). Regardless, most people get the picture.

Technically speaking, the Hebrew translation (properly cited) would not suggest **by** *the skin of my teeth*, but **with** *the skin of my teeth*, which would suggest all Job has left is the shell.

Regardless, the expression speaks to one very narrow escape, which nets us one very colorful expression still referenced today.

Later popularized by the American humorist Thornton Wilder, *Skin of My Teeth* also made its musical debut when the a heavy metal rock group Megadeth referenced the phrase in a 1990s song that had absolutely nothing to do with Scripture.

POOR AS JOB'S TURKEY

Scripture tells us that Job had 7,000 sheep, 3,000 camels, 500 yoke of oxen and 500 donkeys in his happier days, but not one scriptural reference claims he had a turkey.

So who's to credit for this reference so commonly associated with being poorer than poor?

The opening lines of the book of Job describe a holy man who feared God and lived justly. Scripture also tells us he was really wealthy... blessed by God, though his faith was tested when his worldly possessions were taken from him, his family killed, and his body wracked with disease.

(That his name is forever synonymous with a phrase like *Poor as Job's Turkey* is just one more addition to his misery.)

That said, the image of a single, sickly, lowly turkey is nowhere to be found in the sacred texts. Instead Job's Turkey is the invention of 19th century humorist Thomas Haliburton.

According to this Canadian writer, Job's turkey had but one feather and was so weak with hunger he had to prop himself up against a barn just to gobble.

He was pitiful.

But he wasn't scriptural.

Curiously, however, while Job is proverbial for his patience, the Book of Job only depicts him as such for two chapters. The expression "patient as Job" comes not from the Book of Job itself, but from the New Testament book of James, which states:

Behold, we count them happy which endure. Ye have heard of the patience of Job, and have seen the end of the Lord; that the Lord is very pitiful, and of tender mercy.

(James 5:11)

Not to be confused with …

POOR AS A CHURCH MOUSE

...which likewise, isn't scriptural. But the fact that we associate the poor, lowly mouse to something so near our worshipful hearts, well...it kinda makes you wonder, "Why a church mouse? Why not a field mouse or a barn mouse?" and "Do churches even have mice, for goodness sake?"

As expressions go, *poor as a church mouse* traces back to 17th-century England, though some claim the expression finds its roots in German and in French expressions recorded much earlier.

To grasp the concept, think back to those single-room churches of old...the very kind that first peppered our country in the days of the early pioneers.

(Keep in mind that our modern-day churches, with everything from fellowship halls to libraries to gymnasiums, have come a long way from those single-room, clapboard structures built solely, and soulfully, with worship in mind.)

As the village church was the central point to any new township (hence its steeple, which could be seen from miles away), it was likewise one of the few structures that had neither food nor running water on hand, much less the facilities in which to prepare a meal.

Thus to be *poor as a church mouse* means not only that you, yourself, have nothing, but it suggests you don't even have enough sustenance to attract a mouse by way of your crumbs, which is to say, a pretty lowly life, indeed.

OUT OF THE MOUTHS OF BABES

(PSALM 8:2)

Straight from the Bible (and twice, no less) the familiarity of this oft-cited expression lead many to credit Shakespeare.

But it was Jesus who made it noteworthy when quoting the original Psalm, he captured the attention of the chief priests and scribes.

Modern interpretations range from a biblical *"kids say the darndest things"* to the God-like wisdom found in innocence. But to truly understand the phrase, it helps to review. Psalm 8:1-2 states:

O Lord our Lord, how excellent is thy name in all the earth! Who has set thy glory above the heavens. Out of the mouth of babes and sucklings has thou ordained strength because of thine enemies, that thou mightest still the enemy and the avenger.

A song of praise, the psalter uses *out of the mouth of babes* to express God's ability to use even the weakest of creatures to embody God's might.

Jesus' reference to the same, spoken just as the masses are singing his praises, is timely if not cryptic.

Having just rebuked the money-changers in the temple for turning his "house of prayer" into a "den of thieves," Jesus' choice of passage gave pause for thought:

Yea; have ye never read, Out of the mouth of babes and sucklings thou hast perfected praise?

(Matthew 21:16)

With children singing hosanna to the son of David, the scene like the Scripture he references speaks of truth uttered from innocence... a song of praise coming *out of the mouth of babes*.

BITE THE DUST

(PSALM 72:9)

For whatever reason, there is something about dust that brings out the phrase book in writers, which, over time, has netted us a myriad of images involving dirt and oral fixations.

From the most classical of poets to Hollywood's finest screenwriters, we need go no farther than our local video store to find us *biting the dust*, *eating the dust*, and now (thanks to Scripture) even *licking the dust* (which makes this expression *older than dust*, but that's another story).

While *biting the dust* references death (think cowboys falling off horses, face first into the dirt), the earliest recorded dust-tasting activity traces to Psalm 72 where the power and the wisdom of King Solomon are predicted to be so great that nations will bow down.

Specifically, the passage reads:

They that dwell in the wilderness shall bow before him and his enemies shall lick the dust.

Metaphorically speaking, I'll grant you that *licking the dust* is not quite the same as *biting the dust* (as one is a more humbling experience where the other means, well… you croaked).

Still and so, the fact that dust and digestion have been united in our language for thousands of years is, to me,

   … worthy of note.

SWEET HONEY IN THE ROCK

(PSALM 81:16)

For lots of folks, Sweet Honey in the Rock will forever resonate with that a cappella ensemble of African-American women who sing like angels. (FYI and just in case you didn't grow up Church of Christ, *a cappella* means no instruments—just voices.)

So what was the inspiration behind the naming of this Grammy-winning group, you ask?

Well, I shall tell you.

The original reference comes from the book of Psalms, wherein the Scripture reads:

He should have fed them also with the finest of the wheat: and with honey out of the rock should I have satisfied thee.

(Psalm 81:16)

One of our more poetic Psalms (Psalm being the Greek word for "song" by the way), the reference to sweet honey is one of sweetness and all things desirable found in God's natural world (coming from something as hard as a rock, no less).

So you might be thinking by now, "Hey wait! Wasn't Canaan called the land of milk and honey?" (And I would answer by saying, "Why yes, it was.")

But why is this interesting?

Well, it's interesting because biologically speaking, milk and honey are two substances that can replenish themselves naturally (which means they provide nourishment without requiring the death or the harvesting that meat, vegetables and even fruit require).

Sweet, huh?

(AT THEIR) WIT'S END

(PSALM 107:27-28)

An expression as popular today as when it was first penned, a person at his *wit's end* is frazzled... eaten up with worry or exasperation, most likely resulting from repeated attempts to resolve a matter all by himself (but to no avail).

What most don't know is that the first mention of anyone being at this *wit's end* is, indeed, biblical in origin. And again, it hails from the book of Psalms.

Listing a litany of stressful scenarios the expression in its entirety reads:

They reel to and fro, and stagger like a drunken man, and are at their wit's end.

Then they cry unto the Lord in their trouble, and he bringeth them out of their distresses.

So try to absorb the picture here. (Think sea-sick and staggering. That's what being at your wit's end is all about.)

The original references a thanksgiving prayer, as the Psalmist describes the fear of a storm-tossed sailor, miraculously saved by calling on the Lord.

In Biblical color commentary, the writer depicts one seasick scenario, complete with the panic that would ensue.

Interestingly, the Hebrew word for *wit* is more akin to *wisdom*, suggesting that one at the end of such, has reached the end of his reasoning rope.

Some call the verse prophetic—an Old Testament foreshadowing of Jesus' (New Testament) experience involving a boat, his disciples and a storm.

The rocking and reeling is reminiscent of the Old Testament passage, only this story ends with three simple words: *"Peace, be still"* *(Mark 4:39)*.

Spoken by Jesus who calmed the seas, no one on this boat winds up at his *wit's end.*

WOE IS ME

(PSALM 120:5; ISAIAH 6:5; JEREMIAH 4:31)

A word that connotes distress or difficulty, "woe" is synonymous with grief and sorrow.

For instance, in Psalm 120:5 we read: "*Woe is me, that I sojourn in Mesech, that I dwell in the tents of Kedar!*"

In Isaiah 6:5, we read: "*Then said I, Woe is me! For I am undone; because I am a man of unclean lips, and I dwell in the midst of a people of unclean lips: for mine eyes have seen the King, and the Lord of hosts.*"

And in Jeremiah 4:31 we read: "*For I have heard a voice as of a woman in travail, and the anguish of her that bringeth forth her first child, the voice of the daughter of Zion, that bewaileth herself, that spreadeth her hands, saying, Woe is me now! For my soul is wearied because of murderers.*"

In each scenario, the writer speaks of woe as a result of the real world and often wicked conditions that surround him. In other words, it is a sad and distressing state indeed when a righteous person gets stuck living in unrighteous surroundings and with wicked people.

Although "woe is me" may be the most familiar use of the term "woe," in most of its uses in the Bible, "woe" signals the misfortune that will face people who do not behave in a righteous way. For example, Jeremiah 22:13 reads: *"Woe unto him that buildeth his house by unrighteousness, and his chambers by wrong; that useth his neighbour's service without wages, and giveth him not for his work."*

The New Testament uses this same expression. According to Luke 6:24, Jesus states: *"But woe unto you that are rich! for ye have received your consolation."*

The Hebrew term underlying the English "woe" is pronounced "oy"—and in this form it comes into Yiddish, the language of East European Jews.

SPARE THE ROD

(PROVERBS)

While the book of Proverbs provides ample fodder for a phrase too often quoted as Scripture, I'm sorry to report that *spare the rod and spoil the child* is nowhere to be found in the sacred text.

True, there are several references to corporal punishment in Proverbs, but none so poetic (or tidy) as the prose we cite.

In Proverbs 13:24 we find:

He that spareth his rod, hateth his son: but he that loveth him chasteneth him betimes.

In Proverbs 22:15 we find:

Foolishness is bound in the heart of a child; but the rod of correction shall drive it far from him.

And in Proverbs 23:14 we find the more graphic...

SPOIL THE CHILD

(PROVERBS 23:14)

Thou shalt beat him with the rod,
and shalt deliver his soul from hell.

To give credit where credit is due, the poetic and hence more commonly cited expression was the creation of Samuel Butler in his satiric poem, "Hudibras" (1664), wherein it was written:

Love is a boy by poets styl'd;
Then spare the rod and spoil the child.

Curiously, there is another side to the rod, too often equated with all things discipline and punishment.

Let us not forget that rod and staff are symbols of comfort in the oft-cited 23rd Psalm, which reads:

Thy rod and thy staff, they comfort me.

PRIDE GOETH BEFORE A FALL

(PROVERBS 16:18)

Despite the popularity of the proverb *Pride goeth before a fall*, that is not actually what the Bible says. Rather, according to Scripture, *"Pride goeth before destruction…"* (It's that haughty spirit that will knock you off your feet.)

For clarification's sake, the King James Version of this proverb states: *"Pride goeth before destruction, and a haughty spirit before a fall."* The meaning is pretty self explanatory: get arrogant, cocky or overly confident and watch out! You're bound to stumble. The form of the proverb is in what is known as "poetic parallelism"; the first phrase and the second phrase mean the same thing.

But what is it about pride that makes for so many warnings in Scripture? (There are more than two dozen biblical passages pertaining to it.)

One argument is that those who are prideful do not give sufficient credit to God for their accomplishments. A related point is that the prideful do not recognize that they have received help from others. A third view is that prideful people are snobbish and judgmental; they think they are better than everyone else. To be certain, when it comes to personality traits that the Bible approves, humility tops the charts.

The New Testament Epistle of James tells us: "*God resisteth the proud, but giveth grace to the humble*" (James 4:6).

And 1 Peter 5:5 admonishes: "*Be submissive to one another, and be clothed with humility.*"

Or as another proverb so aptly reiterates:

When pride cometh, then cometh shame:
  but with the lowly is wisdom.

(Proverbs 11:2)

TO EVERYTHING . . . THERE IS A SEASON

(ECCLESIASTES 3:1-8)

To Everything …(turn, turn, turn)
There is a Season …(turn, turn, turn)

Who knew we were memorizing Scripture when we were singing along with that 1952 Pete Seeger tune?

The original lyric was ecclesiastical (big word meaning: pertains to church or clergy).

In a nutshell, the prose hails from the Old Testament book of Ecclesiastes, written in the persona of Solomon (though not believed by most scholars to have been literally written by King Solomon himself).

Regardless, this timeless writing is still today some of the purest poetry ever penned.

While open to interpretation, the essence of the tune is one of perspective, placing the elements of life into cycles best viewed not as right or wrong, but more as an ebb and flow to be expected. In its entirety, the Scripture reads:

To every thing there is a season, and a time to every purpose under the heaven:

A time to be born, and a time to die; a time to plant, and a time to pluck up that which is planted;

A time to kill, and a time to heal; a time to break down, and a time to build up;

A time to weep, and a time to laugh; a time to mourn, and a time to dance;

A time to cast away stones, and a time to gather stones together; a time to embrace, and a time to refrain from embracing;

A time to get, and a time to lose; a time to keep, and a time to cast away;

A time to rend, and a time to sew; a time to keep silence, and a time to speak;

A time to love, and a time to hate; a time of war, and a time of peace.

(The line "I swear it's not too late" compliments of Seeger, not Scripture.)

FLY IN THE OINTMENT

(ECCLESIASTES 10:1)

A figure of speech often believed to be folklore rather than Scripture, a *fly in the ointment* suggests that the smallest of improprieties can take down the greater good. (In other words, it only takes the tiniest of annoyances to spoil something of far larger value.)

To be sure, the concept originates with Scripture. First reference to this annoying scenario, we credit to the writer of the Old Testament book of Ecclesiastes. The text in its entirety reads:

Dead flies cause the ointment of the apothecary
*   to send forth a stinking savour;*
*   so doth a little folly him that is*
*   in reputation for wisdom and honor.*

(Ecclesiastes 10:1)

The phrase has been popularized more recently by authors and song writers alike who borrowed this visual imagery in titling their works.

Think of it as the biblical version of "one bad apple" and you're almost there. (And if that Donny Osmond tune by the same name is now playing in your head, don't get angry with me, just feel free to hum along. Ditto that if your favorite rendition was the Jackson Five's.)

The essence of this verse is one and the same...

Whether you're talking spoiled medicines or a sullied reputation, a *fly in the ointment* reminds us that it only takes a little bad to ruin the lot of something good.

DROP IN THE BUCKET

(ISAIAH 40:15)

An expression that is the epitome of "This ain't nothing compared to the big picture," the original passage was spoken by a prophet living in exile, who prophesied to the children of Israel assuring them that their Babylonian captivity would soon come to an end. The passage was another way of saying that in time, the enemy's hold would be but a blip on the radar.

Behold, the nations are as a drop of a bucket, and are counted as the small dust of the balance…

(Isaiah 40:15)

So common is the phrase that people often forget it's scriptural. (Some credit it to secular writings like the Edinburgh Weekly Journal, but this would be short sighted.)

The original was coined by Isaiah reminding the faithful that neither nature nor nations would deter the plan of God.

NO REST FOR THE WEARY

(ISAIAH 57:20-21)

An expression that suggests one must keep on keeping on no matter how tired or overworked, the original is: *no rest for the wicked*, which bears a slightly edgier connotation.

The implication is that the devil never sleeps, nor allows his followers to rest from their plotting and planning.

While the phrase has appeared periodically over the centuries, the original hails from the book of Isaiah, and reads:

But the wicked are like the troubled sea, when it cannot rest, whose waters cast up mire and dirt. There is no peace, saith my God, to the wicked.

(Isaiah 57:20-21)

HOLIER THAN THOU

(ISAIAH 65:5)

Ah…the ol' *Holier than Thou* attitude…You need only hear the words to know precisely what we're talking about. It's one of the few phrases still spoken in the King's English, just for effect.

Other words to describe this attitude:

Self-righteous
>   Pious
>   Sanctimonious
>   Smug

One thing is for certain: you know it when you see it. And most of us would much prefer to distance ourselves from one exhibiting this behavior, for it is a tad hoity toity, only worse, as holier than thou carries a self-righteous air about it. Let's face it: there's nothing worse than spiritual pride.

It is Isaiah who gives us this phrase. Isaiah is condemning people who participate in pagan practices, such as eating swine's flesh and burning incense to foreign gods. These people tell others to stay away from them, lest their holiness be compromised. They tell others, "Stand by thyself, come not near to me; for I am holier than thou."

For the record, this *holier than thou* attitude is noted as one of the more egregious abominations as far as God is concerned. To God, they are said to be...

a smoke in my nose, fire that burneth all the day.

Modern-day interpretation: Think allergens. Think aversions. Think things that get under your skin and into your system that irritate you. Then you've got the picture for how God views those who consider themselves holier than thou.

CAN A LEOPARD CHANGE HIS SPOTS?

Can the Ethiopian change his skin,
or the leopard his spots?
(JEREMIAH 13:23)

Who knew? Yes, this one originates with the Bible. And though often asked rhetorically, the answer to the question is "No. A leopard cannot change its spots."

For the Bible, the citation concerns not outward appearance, but inward attitude.

...Then may ye also do good, that are accustomed to do evil. (Or as newer translations word it: *Neither can you do good, who are accustomed to doing evil.*)

In other words, people simply don't change their natures.

The story of the turtle and the scorpion comes to mind…

A turtle was one day swimming along when a scorpion on the riverbank asks him for a ride to the other shore. Knowing full well that scorpions sting, the turtle rejects the request. But when the scorpion counters by arguing, "If I were to sting you, you would drown, which means I would drown too," the turtle agrees to give the scorpion a ride.

Just as they approach the other shore, the scorpion stings the turtle after all, and when the turtle asks why, the scorpion replies, "Because I'm a scorpion."

As is true for scorpions, is true for leopards, is true (according to Jeremiah) for people of an evil nature. Some things will never change.

(But fortunately, as Matthew 19:26 tells us, …*with God, all things are possible.*)

SOUR GRAPES

(EZEKIEL 18:2)

Mere mention of *Sour grapes* takes most of us back to Aesop's fable of "The Fox and the Grapes," wherein a fox, struggling for grapes high on a vine, gives up while rationalizing, "Those grapes were sour anyway."

Moral being, it's easy to find fault with goals you're never going to attain.

But the phrase turns scriptural when Ezekiel, the prophet, asks God to explain a proverb involving the same. We read:

> *The fathers have eaten sour grapes,*
> *and the children's teeth are set on edge.*

Now we don't know whether Ezekiel is referencing the fable handed down from the time of Aesop. But we do know that certain expressions, told over time, take on new meanings as they are conveyed culture to culture.

In Aesop's case, sour grapes refer to someone rationalizing failure when the goal is not attained.

For Ezekiel, sour grapes spoke to a question of personal responsibility.

In response, God assures Ezekiel that each individual will be judged by his or her own actions... that the sins of the father will not be held against future generations.

Whether related or not, it is interesting to note common elements of fables and proverbs of the day.

And just so you know, fable we take from the Latin word *fabula*, meaning story. Proverbs derives from the Latin word *proverbium*, meaning a story with a moral or lesson. Both were key literary devices used to illustrate a point.

(And just in case you were about to look it up, Aesop was a slave and storyteller, who lived in ancient Greece from 620-560 B.C.)

FEET OF CLAY

(DANIEL 2:31-32)

From the apocalyptic book of Daniel, King Nebuchadnezzar, founder of the new Babylonian empire, dreams a dream in which he sees a giant statue said to have a

...head of fine gold... breast and arms of silver... belly and thighs of brass... legs of iron... feet part of iron and part of clay...

(Daniel 2:32-33)

But in stark contrast to the solid metals of this mighty image, the feet of the statue included clay (hardly foundation material for big statues). Just as Joseph interpreted the dreams of Pharaoh, Daniel interprets the dream of this king, telling Nebuchadnezzar that his earthly kingdom is soon to crumble.

Today *feet of clay* has come to symbolize the human element at the base of even our most powerful leaders, and the ability of that human element to bring a kingdom down. (We see it all the time in politics.)

For King Nebuchadnezzar the dream proved prophetic.

For Christians the dream foreshadows God's kingdom to come—eternal and spiritual... a kingdom not made of earthly elements.

But even beyond Scripture, *feet of clay* is commonly used as the metaphorical reminder that even the loftiest of leaders is capable of flaws.

WRITING ON THE WALL

(DANIEL 5:1-31)

An expression that portends evil, doom or an otherwise bad omen, the (hand) writing on the wall comes from the book of Daniel, where mysterious predictions foretell the demise of the Babylonian empire.

It was King Belshazzar of Babylon who, in drunken party mode, denigrates the sacred vessels removed from Solomon's temple by his father, King Nebuchadnezzar.

In sacrilege he raises the sacred goblets while praising the gods of gold, silver, iron, wood and stone.

But the fun and frivolity come to a screeching halt when the disembodied fingers of a human hand appear mid-air, writing words that only Daniel could interpret.

Rejecting payment or praise, Daniel interprets the mysterious words, warning the king that his folly and blasphemy have cost him his kingdom and his life.

Amazingly, the Bible gives us the actual letters on this mysterious text (in case any among us would care to interpret).

And this is the writing that was written, ME'NE, ME'NE, TE'KEL, U-PHAR'SIN This is the interpretation of the thing:

ME'NE; God hath numbered thy kingdom, and finished it.

TE'KEL; Thou art weighed in the balances, and art found wanting…

PER'ES; Thy kingdom is divided, and given to the Medes and Persians.

(Daniel 5:25-28)

In case you're curious as to the story's ending, Scripture goes on to tell us:

In that night was Belshazzar the king of the Chaldeans slain.

(Daniel 5:30)

NEW TESTAMENT

SALT OF THE EARTH

(MATTHEW 5:13/LUKE 14:34)

An expression that traces straight to the Sermon on the Mount, a person who is *the salt of the earth* is a person who's decent, solid and dependable. The specific reference made by Jesus is found both in Matthew and in Luke.

A universal preservative, salt was an absolute necessity in Jesus' day. The element was known for its life-sustaining qualities.

In addition to preserving meat and flavoring food, salt was so valuable in days of old, that it was often used as currency in and of itself. As a matter of fact, our present word "salary" derives from the Roman word *salarium*, as many Roman soldier were paid in salt, highly valued for its preservative qualities in days pre-refrigeration.

But this is only half the story...

Old Testament references for salt abound.

Leviticus 2:13 instructs that offerings should be seasoned with salt.

Numbers 18:19 makes reference to a "salt covenant" between God and the children of Israel.

Ezekiel 16:4 describes how infants were rubbed in salt for good health.

And the list goes on...

From the land of the Dead (Salt) Sea, salt was not only purifying, it was life-preserving—a stable, solid compound, highly valued.

As salt retains these qualities even today, some suggest Jesus' reference to *salt of the earth* was an admonishment to his followers to season and preserve the world by participating in worldly affairs as opposed to removing themselves from it.

NOT WORTH HIS SALT

Keeping with our salty subject, and now that you are mindful of just how valuable salt was back in Jesus's day, other salty phrases should now make more sense.

For instance, a man *not worth his salt* is a person not worth his salary [*sal*, the Latin word for "salt"]—or in other words, the money you pay him.

Take something *with a grain of salt*, and you're helping to offset the blow of an otherwise exaggerated tale; in other words, you'll be helping someone swallow a story, or digest an otherwise, overblown statement. (E.g., when Jim goes to talking about his children, you're best to take it with a grain of salt, as no one's kids are that perfect.)

To *rub salt in a wound* speaks to the powerful punch that even a grain of salt can pack as an irritant to something already hurting. (E.g., to lose to their team was bad enough, but they didn't have to rub salt in the wound by having us stand beside them for pictures as they held up their trophies.)

To *salt away* something makes reference to savings by way of incremental investments—as in squirreling away money or hoarding up food. (E.g., how she managed to pay her bills *and* salt away a nest egg for her retirement is commendable, indeed.)

And last but not least, if you know someone who's a *salty dog* then you know a person who is perhaps a bit crusty, experienced and has been around the block a time or two. Originally a nautical reference, the first salty dogs were sailors who traveled the high seas (and the salty waters thereof)—sojourners wise to the ways of the world, living a sailor's life of shipboard duties and knowing the ropes.

TURNING THE OTHER CHEEK

(MATTHEW 5:39)

From the Sermon on the Mount, *turning the other cheek* is a familiar expression to most, but a confusing one to many.

Given the parameters of the expression however, this we do know: Jesus was stressing a non-violent response to violence—some would even go so far as to say he was a pacifist.

But unless you know the background of its symbolism, this phrase is easily lost in translation.

From Matthew we read:

You have heard that it hath been said, An eye for an eye, and a tooth for a tooth: But I say unto you, That ye resist not evil: but whosoever shall smite thee on thy right cheek, turn to him the other also.

For starters, standing firm in the face of an attacker is probably the last reaction most would expect given the scenario. The biological if not logical response to one hitting you on the face would be anything but sticking around (much less offering another cheek), as most would have an immediate reflex to strike back.

But given the parameters of the situation, we have clues as to what Jesus meant. A slap to the right cheek suggests a back-handed slap (i.e., a slap of dismissal). In turning the other cheek, you force your assailant to use an open palm, which would say, "If you're going to hit me, at least treat me as an equal."

Be it master to slave, husband to wife, Roman to Jew, *turning the other cheek* is about standing up to injustice by forcing your assailant to confront you as an equal in a situation that was otherwise designed to be demeaning.

GOING THE EXTRA MILE

(MATTHEW 5:41)

Straight from the Sermon on the Mount, *going the extra mile* means you are to do more than is expected or demanded of you.

Specifically, the Scripture states:

And whosoever shall compel thee to go a mile, go with him twain…

To understand the Scripture it helps to consider the context of what it means to be in a country under foreign (in this case Roman) occupation.

Picture this—soldiers toting packs weighing 65 to 85 pounds (not counting weapons).

Rule of the day held that a soldier could force any civilian to carry his pack, but only for a mile.

With mile markers at every turn, this was easy enough to track. Thus the civilian that would dare go an extra mile would be altering the equation entirely.

For starters, if the pack were carried even one extra mile (by the civilian), the soldier would be in violation of military codes, placing the civilian in a curious, if not powerful position.

In other words, there are man's laws, and there are God's, and by going beyond what worldly laws would dictate, you offset the balance of power as measured by earthly terms. In short, it alters the power from those oppressing you.

In giving your oppressor what would otherwise only be taken by force, the very notion of power is turned upside down.

WHEN THE LEFT HAND DOESN'T KNOW WHAT THE RIGHT HAND IS DOING

(MATTHEW 6:3)

Contrasting and comparing the motives between hypocrites (from the Greek word, *hypokrisis*, meaning "play acting") and those otherwise driven by selfless motives, Matthew speaks repeatedly (and staunchly) against those whose intentions are not pure.

The reference to the *left hand not knowing what the right hand is doing* alludes to giving for the virtue of giving alone and not for credit or praise.

In a nutshell, the expression means: *Give and get on with it!*

The Scripture in its entirety reads:

But when thou doest alms, let not thy left hand know what thy right hand doeth.

(Matthew 6:3)

In business, the phrase is often equated with keeping one's affairs separate.

In government, the expression carries a more negative, connotation, suggesting the support of counter motives (like supporting gun control laws while funding the NRA).

But in scriptural context, the expression is pure and simple... True giving requires no audience.

PEARLS BEFORE SWINE

(MATTHEW 7:6)

An expression that suggests you might not want to bring out the fine china for those incapable of appreciating it, the Scripture in its entirety reads:

> *Give not that which is holy unto the dogs,*
> *neither cast ye your pearls before swine,*
> *lest they trample them under their feet,*
> *and turn again and rend you.*

(Matthew 7:6)

Spoken by Jesus in the Sermon on the Mount, the analogy is made richer when you consider that in Jewish culture pigs were the ultimate symbol of unclean, and hence, the lowest of low.

By way of this reference to pigs and pearls, Jesus admonishes his disciples to be mindful of their audience.

When it comes to sharing their jewel of a message, they are best sticking to receptive audiences and those who are genuinely open to the message.

In contrasting images of precious pearls and unclean swine, Jesus is saying,

"Don't offer up your finest to those incapable of appreciating it."

WOLF IN SHEEP'S CLOTHING

(MATTHEW 7:15)

A metaphor for an enemy who pretends to be your friend, a *wolf in sheep's clothing* is another classic from the Sermon on the Mount.

But it was an Aesop fable (dating back to the sixth century B.C.) that made metaphor of the phrase centuries earlier. The story is that of a hungry wolf that discovers a sheep's fleece on the ground. By draping himself in it, the wolf finds a covert way to get closer to his prey (i.e., those unsuspecting sheep)!

In scriptural context, a similar image is depicted in the passage:

Beware of false prophets, which come to you in sheep's clothing, but inwardly they are ravening wolves.

As wandering prophets with varying messages were commonplace in the towns and villages of Jesus' day, the admonition was quite simple:

Beware the messenger.

But to help you know your sheep from your wolves, Jesus also offers the ultimate test for spotting false prophets when in the next verse he said:

Ye shall know them by their fruits.

(Matthew 7:16)

A HOUSE DIVIDED AGAINST ITSELF WILL NOT STAND

(MATTHEW 12:25; MARK 3:25; LUKE 11:17)

The notion of a house divided comes to us from Scripture and is a phrase attributed to Jesus. When accused by some Pharisees of casting out demons in the name of Beelzebub, the prince of demons, Jesus responds by simply pointing to its illogical conclusion: the notion of Satan doing a good—by casting out demons—would be Satan working against his own, which in the end, would make for the end of Satan.

As the Gospel of Mark puts it: "*And if a kingdom be divided against itself, that kingdom cannot stand. And if a house be divided against itself, that house cannot stand. And if Satan rise up against himself, and be divided, he cannot stand, but has an end.*"

The expression gained new recognition when cited by Abraham Lincoln in his Senatorial debate against Stephen Douglas in 1858.

At issue: slavery.

Lincoln maintained that the United States could not remain split between those states that recognized the legality of owning slaves and those that did not. In short, a consummate house divided; in this case, the house was our country.

Historic was his speech, which opened with the familiar passage:

"A house divided against itself cannot stand. I believe this government cannot endure, permanently half slave and half free. I do not expect the Union to be dissolved—I do not expect the house to fall—but I do expect it will cease to be divided. It will become all one thing, or all the other. Either the opponents of slavery, will arrest the further spread of it, and place it where the public mind shall rest in the belief that it is in course of ultimate extinction; or its advocates will push it forward, till it shall become alike lawful in all the states, old as well as new—North as well as South."

As history attests, Lincoln was correct: the Civil War (i.e., the War between the States) became the modern example of a house divided.

(HAVING SOMEONE'S) HEAD ON A PLATTER

(MATTHEW 14:6-11)

It's the fate of John the Baptist, son of Elizabeth, cousin of Jesus, that is the source for this expression.

The gospel of Matthew recounts John's outspoken criticism of the marriage of King Herod (the tetrarch) to his brother's wife Herodias, which landed John in prison.

But when Salome (daughter of Herodias) pleases Herod (her uncle-turned-step-dad) with her delightful dance performance, she is granted one wish.

Rather than go for the gold, Salome defers to her mother who's been peeved at John from the get-go. Knowing the king wanted to kill John but feared the crowd's response, Herodias makes her one wish: John's head on a platter.

(Now to be sure, you won't find Salome's name anywhere in the Bible. Instead, it is found in the writings of the first-century historian, Josephus. But meanwhile, back to the story…)

Herod, committed to his promise (spoken in front of dinner guests, no less), orders the beheading.

Before the birthday meal is through, the head of John the Baptist (on a silver platter) is presented to young Salome, who in turn, re-gifts it to her mother.

As a result, *having someone's head on a platter* today suggests the ultimate act of revenge.

If all this sounds familiar, well… the story is the same one upon which Oscar Wilde based his play, Salome.

Dance of the Seven Veils was never called this in Scripture. Instead, the name of the dance first appeared in the notes to Wilde's 1891 stage production.

BLIND LEADING THE BLIND

(MATTHEW 15:14)

An expression you hear quite often in everyday conversation, the *blind leading the blind* depicts an all-too-common scenario. (Think of incompetent leaders, knowing no more than their followers, who try to lead anyway, and you've got the gist.)

The phrase is credited to Jesus and referenced in the gospel of Matthew.

However, to give credit where credit is due, the concept pre-dates Matthew's account, tracing back as far as the seventh century B.C., where, in sacred Hindu texts we find a similar reference.

From the Bible, we read:

Let them alone: they be blind leaders of the blind. And if the blind lead the blind, both shall fall into the ditch.

From the Katha Upanishad:

"Abiding in the midst of ignorance, thinking themselves wise and learned, fools go aimlessly hither and thither, like blind led by the blind."

There's nothing worse than someone who doesn't understand, trying to explain as if he does, to others who are equally ignorant. Then again, we see it all the time...

(Only most folks call it politics!)

BLOOD MONEY

(MATTHEW/ACTS)

Blood money refers to money paid for killing someone. And even in present-day legal terms, the reference is one of money paid by a murderer to the family of the victim. However, this concept is slightly different from the source often credited the phrase.

To be clear, the phrase, *blood money*, is nowhere in the Bible, though the concept of money paid in exchange for (innocent) blood we do find in Matthew's account of Judas' death:

Then Judas, which had betrayed him, when he saw that he was condemned, repented himself, and brought again the thirty pieces of silver to the chief priests and elders.

Saying I have sinned in that I have betrayed the innocent blood. And they said, What is that to us? See thou to that.

And he cast down the pieces of silver in the temple, and departed, and went and hanged himself.

And the chief priests took the silver pieces and said, It is not lawful for to put them into the treasury, because it is the price of blood.

And they took counsel, and bought with them the potter's field, to bury strangers in.

Wherefore that field was called, The field of blood, unto this day.

(Matthew 27:3-8)

Additional insight to the Judas story can be found in chapter one of the book of Acts (18-19). From this account, and specifically the field called Aceldama (translated field of blood), do we derive our concept of *blood money* today.

BURNING THE MIDNIGHT OIL

(MATTHEW 25:6-10)

Not to be confused with burning the candle at both ends, *burning the midnight oil* can, in fact, refer to one who works well into the night...

But scripturally the meaning goes much deeper, having to do with being ever prepared for the return of the Messiah. (Again to be clear, the actual phrase is nowhere to be found in the Bible.)

In the parable of the ten virgins, Jesus likens the kingdom of heaven to ten virgins: five wise, five foolish.

The latter took no oil for their lamps while the wise (like good Girl Scouts) were always prepared.

From the book of Matthew we read:

And at midnight there was a cry made, Behold, the bridegroom cometh; go ye out to meet him. Then all those virgins arose, and trimmed their lamps. And the foolish said unto the wise, Give us of your oil; for our lamps are gone out. But the wise answered, saying, Not so; lest there be not enough for us and you: but go ye rather to them that sell, and buy for yourselves. And while they went to buy, the bridegroom came; and they that were ready went in with him to the marriage: and the door was shut.

(Matthew 25:6-10)

A passage synonymous with eternal preparation, the story is a reminder to be in a perpetual state of readiness for the Lord's return.

OH YE OF LITTLE FAITH

(MATTHEW 8:25-26; MATTHEW 14:30-31;
LUKE 12:27-28)

Spoken in religious context the phrase is a rebuke for one who is lacking in faith. Spoken in secular context the expression has become a humorous response to one whose beliefs (if not abilities) are in question.

Either way, the scriptural chiding in biblical context comes several times and is always spoken by Jesus to those near him who never quite grasp the true power of his divinity. Classic examples include:

Matthew's account of Jesus calming the storm, and his panicked disciples...

And his disciples came to him, and awoke him, saying, Lord, save us: we perish.

And he saith unto them, Why are ye fearful, O ye of little faith? Then he arose, and rebuked the winds and the seas; and there was great calm.

(Matthew 8:25-26)

Peter's attempt to walk on water (wherein he momentarily lapses into disbelief), as the Scripture states...

But when he saw the wind boisterous, he was afraid; and beginning to sink, he cried, saying, "Lord, save me."

And immediately Jesus stretched forth his hand, and caught him, and said unto him, O thou of little faith, wherefore didst thou doubt?

(Matthew 14:30-31)

And Luke's account, wherein Jesus states...

Consider the lilies how they grow: they toil not, they spin not; and yet I say unto you, that Solomon in all his glory was not arrayed like one of these.

If then God so clothe the grass, which is to day in the field, and to morrow is cast into the oven; how much more will he clothe you, O ye of little faith?

(Luke 12:27-28)

THE SPIRIT IS WILLING, BUT THE FLESH IS WEAK

(MATTHEW 26:41; MARK 14:38)

The spirit is willing, but the flesh is weak is an expression that today we tie to everything from diet attempts to moral behaviors. It suggests while we may desire one thing, too often our human frailties prevail, keeping us from reaching the intended result.

In its original context, there is perhaps no more gripping phrase in all of Scripture, as it comes within the graphic depiction of Jesus' darkest hours.

The setting: Gethsemane

The scene: Jesus, knowing his time is at hand, praying fervently to his Father

The cast: Jesus, Peter, James and John

In the story, Jesus has shared his Last Supper with his disciples, and he has come to Gethsemane, on the Mount of Olives, to pray one final time before he will be led to his execution. Gripping is the prayer he offers up in anguish, as he knows the painful road that lies before him. He has asked three of his disciples to stay awake while he prays, but despite their best efforts, they keep falling asleep. The first time it happens, Jesus asks Peter, "What? Could you not watch with me one hour?" after which he tells his disciple:

Watch and pray, that ye enter not into temptation: the spirit indeed is willing, but the flesh is weak.

Jesus knew of and allowed for the human frailties of his disciples. After returning a third time from his impassioned, prayerful state, Scripture tells us the came to his disciples one final time and said:

Sleep on now, and take your rest: behold, the hour is at hand, and the Son of man is betrayed into the hands of sinners.

(Matthew 26:45)

WASHING MY HANDS
OF THE MATTER

(MATTHEW 27:24)

An expressive way to dismiss a matter as no longer your responsibility, the words are spoken in the final stages of Jesus' arrest and crucifixion by Pontius Pilate.

When the crowds yell, *"Crucify him,"* Pilate resists. Warned by his wife (per a dream) that he should have no part in Jesus' death, he is personally conflicted as he asks, *"What evil has he done?"*

But the mob persists. And Scripture states that Pilate

...took water, and washed his hands before the multitude, saying, I am innocent of the blood of this just person: see ye to it.

This pivotal moment in Pilate's life is today a catch phrase, synonymous with removing oneself from a situation entirely.

BAPTISM BY FIRE

(MATTHEW 3:11; LUKE 3:16; ACTS 2:3-4)

Often credited to a French reference to the first fire of the battlefield, the original *baptism by fire* took place in the days following Jesus' resurrection. Acts 2:3-4 describes the scene:

And there appeared unto them cloven tongues like as of fire, and it sat upon each of them. And they were all filled with the Holy Ghost, and began to speak with other tongues, as the Spirit gave them utterance.

From the Greek: *baptisma pyros*, this fire baptism became the symbol for martyrs throughout antiquity.

For Christians since, it represents the baptism of the Holy Spirit, foretold by John the Baptist in Matthew 3:11 and in Luke 3:16.

For everyone else, the expression *baptism by fire* means your mettle has been tested. (A pun of sorts considering that fire is how we test metals on earth!)

GIVE UP THE GHOST

(MARK 15:37; LUKE 23:46;
JOHN 19:30; ACTS 12:23)

To give up the ghost means you died. Given that we use it so nonchalantly these days to describe cowboys in westerns or machinery that quits, it is easy to overlook the sensitive origins of the phrase's first use.

Mark (15:37), Luke (23:46) and John (19:30) all cite the phrase verbatim when recounting the final moment of Jesus' crucifixion.

The same phraseology is referenced once again in the gory depiction of King Herod's death as recounted in Acts 12:23.

Though vastly different circumstances, what is consistent is the graphic detail that accompanies each reference to the phrase. This leaves one to ponder just when *giving up the ghost* became little more than a trivial catchphrase (for in Scripture, it was anything but).

TWINKLING OF AN EYE

(I CORINTHIANS 15:52)

In an expression somewhat Disney-esque, something that happens *in the twinkling of an eye* is an event that connotes magic... like falling in love: it just happens in an instant.

Spiritually speaking, we can thank the apostle Paul, who in describing the resurrection, poetically coined the turn of phrase.

In a moment, in the twinkling of an eye, at the last trump: for the trumpet shall sound, and the dead shall be raised incorruptible, and we shall be changed.

As if the expression weren't mystical enough, this *twinkling of an eye* is one of the few we can trace both to Scripture and to Shakespeare, as the Bard himself adapted the same in his Merchant of Venice, wherein he writes,

"I'll take my leave of the Jew in the twinkling of an eye..." *(Act 2, Scene 2)*.

THORN IN THE FLESH

(II CORINTHIANS 12:7)

A prickly depiction of something that agitates, a *thorn in the flesh* is something (or someone) that perpetually annoys.

Written by the apostle Paul in his second letter to the church in Corinth, the text in its entirety reads:

And lest I should be exalted above measure through the abundance of the revelations, there was given to me a thorn in the flesh, the messenger of Satan to buffet me, lest I should be exalted above measure.

Though Paul prays repeatedly for its removal, he concludes God allows his thorn as a constant reminder of God's grace.

To this day scholars speculate as to what (or who) Paul's thorn really was. Theories range from spiritual temptation to physical handicaps to mental illness. But while the actual thorn is never identified, the expression serves to remind that even God's holiest have their frailties.

SAME OL' SIXES AND SEVENS

A phrase credited to everyone from Chaucer to Shakespeare, *to be at sixes and sevens* means you're in a state of disarray. Trace it further and you find that yes, the original sixes and sevens are both scriptural and symbolic within the text.

To be sure the book of Revelation is laden with sixes and sevens, with sixes representing all things worldly. (Think mark of the beast Revelation [16:2] and you start to get the gist.)

On the other hand, the number seven (first noted as God's divine day of rest) is symbolic of all things perfect. There are seven seals, seven scrolls, seven trumpets, seven bowls... in fact sevens are referenced more than seven times seven (49) in this book alone.

While the book of Revelation attaches great symbolism to both sixes and sevens, the original quote came from the book of Job wherein we read,

He shall deliver thee in six troubles: yea, in seven there shall no evil touch thee.

(Job 5:19)

LABOR OF LOVE

(HEBREWS 6:10; I THESSALONIANS 1:3)

A beautiful turn of phrase, a *labor of love* describes any work done for the love and satisfaction of that work rather than for monetary reward or material gain.

The phrase is found twice in the King James Version of Scripture:

For God is not unrighteous to forget your work and labour of love, which ye have shewed toward his name, in that ye have ministered to the saints, and do minister.

(Hebrews 6:10)

and

Remembering without ceasing your work of faith, and labour of love, and patience of hope in our Lord Jesus Christ, in the sight of God and our Father...

(I Thessalonians 1:3)

In scriptural context, these labors of love refer to the loving works of the early followers of Jesus, specifically those serving as leaders in the first churches whose activities helped support and strengthen the newly emerging communities.

Today the expression reaches far broader into our everyday language; it refers to any task done for sheer love of the work as opposed to work done grudgingly or for ulterior motives.

Curiously, the original meaning behind the word amateur carries a similar connotation, as the first amateurs (from the Latin *amator*, meaning "lover") were likewise those who took on a pastime (such as a craft) out of love for the art form, as opposed to undertaking the task professionally, as a work for hire.

GOD HELPS THOSE
WHO HELP THEMSELVES

(HEZEKIAH 6:1)

In case you're looking for the Scripture on this one, don't bother. (Somebody out there suggested you'll find it in the fictional book of Hezekiah, but since that isn't a real book you could find yourself digging awhile. Just keeping you on your toes!)

Instead, of your Bible, you might consult your almanac (as in Poor Richard's Almanac), as most credit Benjamin Franklin for at least popularizing this oft mis-attributed quote (a quote that suggests that self-initiative is a key element when it comes to those who receive God's help).

Dig a little deeper and you'll discover that the phrase wasn't original with Benjamin Franklin. The notion that we should meet divine powers halfway dates all the way back to Greek antiquity, as one sage stated:

"Along with Athena, move also your hand."

The first use of the familiar English proverb we trace to Algernon Sydney's *198 Discourses Concerning Government* (a treaty challenging the monarchy that cost Sydney his life). Variations on the same theme have been carried down through generations and from culture to culture.

Ironically, as some have pointed out, the Bible often presents exactly the opposite teaching: we are to depend on God and not on ourselves.

But as phrases go, *God helps those who help themselves* is, perhaps, *the* most often quoted Scripture *never* found in the Bible. (So go ahead. Impress your friends. Just don't get *holier than thou* about it.)

GOD BLESS YOU

While the Good Book is full of blessings, you'll be hard pressed to find the words *God Bless You* written verbatim anywhere, and you certainly won't find it prescribed as a prayer to say when someone sneezes.

Scripturally speaking, the closest words resembling this simple prayer are found in Numbers, where in chapter 6, verses 24 -26, we read:

The Lord bless thee, and keep thee: The Lord make his face shine upon thee, and be gracious unto thee: The Lord lift up his countenance upon thee, and give thee peace.

No more beautiful prayer was ever uttered. No more poetic words ever penned.

But if this is the Bible's version of God's direct blessing, who came up with *God Bless You*, and who (dare pray) assigned it as customarily to be uttered when someone sneezes out loud?

History for the custom itself predates the Bible, for long ago, ancient spiritual beliefs held that a person's soul could exit the body under certain stressful conditions (be they physical or emotional). It was furthermore believed that on such occasions, a person could find his soul literally outside of his own body, given the right set of conditions. (This notion also gives rise to our expression of being "beside oneself"; e.g., *"She was so livid that he had not called… why, she was simply beside herself!"*)

As for *God Bless You*, one such situation that could bring about the blessing was the common cold where it was believed that if a sneeze were strong enough, a person could literally blast his spirit right out of his body!

In such an event, this little, but powerful prayer was believed to protect the empty shell until the soul (i.e., its rightful owner) could re-enter.

To ensure that evil spirits did not move in during the vacancy, *God Bless You* was said to keep the temple clean, so soul and body could reunite once again.

THE ALPHA

Alpha and Omega. First and last. Beginning and end. An alphabetical metaphor for a name that is just too large for letters, the Alpha and Omega are mentioned several times in the book of Revelation in symbolism of the end all, be all, eternal nature of God.

I am Alpha and Omega, the beginning and the ending, saith the Lord, which is, and which was, and which is to come, the Almighty.

(Revelation 1:8)

Most know these are the first and last letters of the Greek alphabet. But dig a little deeper and more mystical facets of these two letters come into play.

For example, in addition to being the first and last letters of the Greek alphabet, Alpha and Omega are also both vowels.

. . . AND OMEGA

(So why would this matter, you ask? Well, here's where things get interesting.)

Certain Greek mystery traditions held that vowels possessed life. Just as air brings life into a body, so too did vowels breathe life into a word.

According to such traditions, these vowels (when strung together as one word) possessed the very energy and essence of God.

Chanted in sacred combination, one could tap God's divine vibration according to the mystics.

With or without the mystery schools, Alpha and Omega are synonymous still with the endless, timeless, supremacy of God.

ABOUT THE AUTHOR

Karlen Evins is a writer, producer and talk show host with a journalism career that spans twenty years. A communications graduate from the University of Tennessee, she received her Masters in Theological Studies from Vanderbilt University in 2004.

When she isn't writing, Karlen serves as an advocate for the homeless, both as a volunteer and as President of the Board for Nashville's Room in the Inn. A lifelong Tennessean, she lives with her 3 dogs, one very spoiled cat, and 16 pygmy goats.

Creator of the Southern to the Core series of cookbooks and video productions, Karlen loves farming, renovating houses, yoga and meditation. Her latest passion is growing and harvesting lavender.